RAVE REVIEWS FOR LEO HAUSER'S

FIVE STEPS TO SUCCESS
The Biggest Little Book You'll Ever Read!

"The 'meat and potatoes' found in your FIVE STEPS TO SUC-CESS will feed us for a lifetime."
—**Bart Starr**

"Your FIVE STEPS TO SUCCESS is a very important part of opening doors to new thinking and learning for our members."
—**Charlotte Tharp, President, American Women in Radio and Television**

"YOUR FIVE STEPS TO SUCCESS is an inspiration to all entrepreneurs, small business people, and those considering starting their own business. Thank you."
—**John Black, General Manager, Control Data Business & Technology Centers**

"FIVE STEPS TO SUCCESS is exactly what students need in today's world to ensure they maximize their full potentials in school, career, and life. Thanks, Leo, for sharing them with our members."
—**Dwight Loken, Associate Director, Office Education Association**

"FIVE STEPS TO SUCCESS is the heart that pumps blood to the bone and sinew of every enterprise."
—**Ron Zemke, Research Editor, *Training Magazine***

"Leo Hauser spread a 'Can Do' message that inspires others. Successful people, he says, have mastered self-control and there-fore their options for success are tremendous."
—**Robert Speck, Financial Editor, *Toledo Blade***

FIVE STEPS TO SUCCESS

Leo Hauser

BERKLEY BOOKS, NEW YORK

This Berkley book contains the complete text
of the original edition.

FIVE STEPS TO SUCCESS

A Berkley Book / published by arrangement with
the author

PRINTING HISTORY
Hauser Productions edition published 1984
Berkley edition / November 1991

ISBN: 0-425-13036-3

A BERKLEY BOOK ® TM 757,375
Berkley Books are published by The Berkley Publishing Group,
200 Madison Avenue, New York, New York 10016.
The name "Berkley" and the "B" logo
are trademarks belonging to Berkley Publishing Corporation.

PRINTED IN THE UNITED STATES OF AMERICA

10 9 8 7 6 5 4 3 2

To my wonderful wife, Helen, and three children: Polo, Libby, and Sara, in thanks for the mutual love and respect we have shared over the years

CONTENTS

WORK PAGES

STEP ONE — GET TO KNOW YOURSELF

STEP TWO — PICK THE RIGHT OPPORTUNITY

STEP THREE — SET BIG GOALS FOR YOURSELF

STEP FOUR — WORK

STEP FIVE — HAVE FUN

PREFACE

This book has been coming together in my mind for years. I've thought about it, talked about it in speeches all over the world, and written about it in magazine and newsletter articles.

As I explain in more detail later in this book, I developed a great hunger for success. Eventually I discovered ways to reach my goals. I applied what I learned through several different careers and had exciting results. I'm still amazed at how simple and reliable these principles are.

And now, because I've received so much from so many other people, I feel it's about time I put a few beans back into the barrel.

After years of helping my employees reach their goals and hearing their grateful response to my suggestions, I decided that what I had learned was important enough to share with lots of other people in all walks of life.

So for the past 13 years, I've been presenting the principles behind the FIVE STEPS TO SUCCESS in speeches to audiences throughout the world. And whether those in attendance were executives, entrepreneurs, farmers, salespeople, government employees, parents, religious leaders, or students, and whether they were in New York, Des Moines, Singapore, or New Delhi, they all asked the same question.

"Do you have these principles in a book so I can review them and build them into my life?"

Also during these years I've received many grateful letters from individuals who learned my FIVE STEPS TO SUCCESS and then wrote to me with exciting news on how success had come into their lives as a result of them.

This has been thrilling for me and it's provided additional credibility to the principles behind the FIVE STEPS TO SUCCESS. It's also given me additional information to use in writing this book.

Over the years, as Publisher of the Self-development Journal and Publisher and Editor of my quarterly newsletter, Successfully Yours, I've expanded on various aspects of these five steps. This too has given me further documentation for this book.

And now, at last, I've finally forced myself to gather into one place all the information and research I've absorbed over the years on the subject of success. I've gone over it, sorted it out, and put it into book form.

I've worked hard to keep this book short, simple, and to the point. I'm a person who likes to meet an issue head-on, make the necessary decisions, and move into action. I assume you do too. If I'm right, then this book is for you.

So welcome aboard and let's get started.

Leo Hauser

INTRODUCTION: What Is a Leo Hauser?

LEO HAUSER is a man who speaks with experience. At the age of 28 he was National Product Manager for General Mills. He then entered the securities field and within five years purchased his own seat on the New York Stock Exchange! At the age of 35 he sold his seat on the Exchange to devote full time to helping others realize their true dimensions in life.

His progress in achieving these objectives has been recognized throughout the world. Leo was elected President of the American Society for Training and Development (over 20,000 U.S. Trainers) and President of the International Federation of Training and Development Organizations (the highest position of any American to achieve in the training field), centered in Geneva, Switzerland.

Leo has been on the Steering Committee for the U.S. Department of Education Life-Long Learning Committee, the Editorial Advisory Board for Training Magazine, Publisher of the Self-Development Journal, co-owner of a bank, a member of the National Speakers' Association, Editor and Publisher of the Successfully Yours quarterly newsletter and is on the Board of Directors of four companies.

As co-founder of Personal Dynamics Institute, Leo was the guiding force behind this international organization, which has conducted seminars in 18 countries and 7 foreign languages (more than 350,000 people throughout the world have experienced Adventures In Attitudes) and it was established as the fastest-growing seminar in the world at that time.

Leo's speeches, cassette tapes and writings have been received enthusiastically in countries all over the world.

Read carefully and listen closely, because here's a man who has used these principles with extraordinary results in 3 separate careers —a man who truly WALKS THE TALK!

YOU'RE MY KIND
OF PERSON

You're my kind of person. Why? Because you're taking the time to stop for a minute, to step back from your work and from building your part of the great American dream, and you're asking yourself, "What can I do to get better at what I'm doing?"

You're my kind of person because you're taking the time to sharpen your axe, fuel your fire, or do whatever you need to do to develop the successful edge. You know you need that edge when you go back to your office, kitchen, garage, church, factory, school, or wherever it is that you're hewing the stones and mixing the mortar of your success.

This is not a long, dull, and boring book. There are two reasons for that. For one thing, I don't want to keep you away from your desk, workbench, or laboratory any longer than necessary. I want to keep you just long enough

1.

to give you some simple but powerful tools for making your dreams of success come true.

EVERYONE NEEDS YOU

You're my kind of person, and I don't want to interrupt your progress toward success for anything. We need you too badly. Our economy needs you. Our country needs you. Our government needs you.

Why do we need you? Because nothing will happen in this country until people like you in some way create new value, service, wealth, energy, or vision that will get us moving ahead. Nothing will happen in our economy until people like you find new ways of living and working that are better and cheaper than what we have right now. And nothing will happen in our schools and churches until people like you are better at getting other people committed to their goals and dreams.

So read fast, and don't sleep any more than you have to. Because if this country, our way of life, or the whole world ever needed the leadership, vitality, and entrepreneurial fervor that people like you represent, it's right now. God bless you and keep it up.

Another reason why this is a short book is that the rules and tools of success are few and simple. They're easy to explain, easy to write about, and easy to understand. And they're easy to adopt to your business, service, or vocation. They do not, however, constitute a magic cure. Nor do they promise overnight success. There are no magic jelly beans in this jar.

The FIVE STEPS TO SUCCESS I want to share with you give you a beacon you can use to light your pathway to success. But you still have to roll up your sleeves, bend your back, and keep moving on down the road of life to reach the success you dream of.

No one I know ever had a treasure ship come in without first sending a venture ship out to sea. But I truly believe that the FIVE STEPS TO SUCCESS will keep your life on the right track. You'll do the right work, and you'll do it as effectively and efficiently as possible. The five steps will also help you get as much from your effort as possible. I also believe that these five steps will help you enjoy the striving as well as the arriving, the journey as well as the destination.

Let me clarify one thing before we jump into the process I call the FIVE STEPS TO SUCCESS. These are *not* Leo Hauser's very own five steps. I didn't sit down one day in a surge of inspiration and carve them out of marble. Not at all. I saw them working in the lives of other successful people. Then I put them to work for myself. And believe me, if they've worked for me, they'll certainly work for you.

Just to clarify this point, I want to share some of the holes in my socks with you. I grew up in St. Paul, Minnesota, where I had the great distinction of being one of the poorest kids in the richest neighborhood in town. And I was anything but a superstar. That was especially true of my performance in school.

I'm not proud of this, you understand, but the fact remains that with a good tail wind, I barely managed to be a C student. But I'll tell you what I had going for me. I had a father who believed anything was possible and who cared enough to share that belief in a loving and compassionate way with his son.

I grew up in the shadow of the great depression. My dad worked down at the post office, and more than once he would come home, eat, change clothes, and go right out to another job just to make ends meet. But the fact that he had to work so hard for so little didn't dampen his spirit in the slightest.

That great big old German would set me on his knee (and when you're five years old, and your dad is that big, it's like being in the hands of God), and he'd say, "Leo, this is America. It's everybody's responsibility to do better than the previous generation."

Now that's quite a charge to give a five-year old who's still having trouble tying his shoes. But my dad really believed what he said. And who was I to doubt this gentle giant.

In light of my humble beginnings and mediocre school performance, I can't honestly say that I saw myself as being successful. That would be stretching it. But my dad did get me interested in becoming successful. So early on, I got curious about the people in the Horatio Alger stories he told me. I started reading about the great men of our country; John D. Rockefeller, Thomas Edison, James J. Hill, and many others.

It wasn't until I went to the University of Minnesota and majored in business that I really got excited about learning for the first time. There I was, in college, reading about my idols all over again. All those industrial giants were reintroduced in the business courses I was taking. I was meeting them again, and getting academic credit at the same time. It was great.

The formula for their success is the same formula I learned and used. And it's a formula that knows no age limits. It's the formula that worked for me at age thirty, for Henry Kaiser at age thirteen, and the same one that worked for sixty-six year old Harland Sanders.

I'm sure you know about the "Colonel's" incredible success story. It's an entrepreneurial classic.

Harland Sanders had worked for years to build a thriving restaurant and motel business. Then the highway on which he had built his business was rerouted, and literally put him out of business. He had to sell everything at auction just to raise enough money to cover his debts.

But Colonel Sanders wasn't about to give up and retire on government hand-outs. So he packed up his old '46 Ford, grabbed his beloved pressure cooker, fifty pounds of his special (now famous) seasoning with its secret herbs and spices, and began his tireless journey from restaurant to restaurant.

The Colonel talked to owners and chefs and anyone else who'd listen to him. He would fry up a batch of chicken and get them to agree that it was indeed "finger-licking-good." Then he'd offer to sell them his special seasoning and teach them his unusual cooking method.

Harland Sanders started driving and cooking and making that sales pitch in Kentucky. Then, with no success at all, he headed west. He didn't make his first sale until he reached Salt Lake City. The restaurant owner in Salt Lake who bought the Colonel's chicken recipe went on to become the first of several hundred millionaires in the Kentucky Fried Chicken business. And of course the Colonel went on to become more rich and famous than all of them.

What I'm telling you here in black and white, is that Colonel Harland Sanders, Henry J. Kaiser, John D. Rockefeller, and every other successful person I've read about, talked with, and listened to, followed the same five steps I'm giving you in this book. Athletes, actors, religious leaders, business people, and homemakers have all taken these FIVE STEPS TO SUCCESS and built them into their life style. These same steps have led me to personal and professional success, and they'll do the same for you.

Are you ready? Do you want to reach the levels of success you've always dreamed about? If you do, then let's get started with Step Number One.

STEP ONE
GET TO KNOW YOURSELF

This step seems awfully simple, doesn't it? But it sometimes takes more work than you might think.

What I want you to do is take an honest-to-goodness, objective look at yourself. Look back on your life and identify all those things you liked to do, especially the things you were good at and got good results from. Then look back at the things you didn't like to do. Your experience will probably show that those things didn't work out so well for you.

The comparison between things you liked to do and didn't like to do is important. Because if you liked doing something and were good at it, you probably did it with enthusiasm and were successful. Conversely, if you did something you didn't like to do, you probably did it as little as possible, were not good at it, and came up with poor results.

So the first step in the FIVE STEPS TO SUCCESS is to discover what you're good at and like to do. You want to identify your talents, skills, and abilities, because they're going to propel you to greatness. At the same time, you have to know what your weaknesses are no matter how hard they are to admit to. Because in order to move ahead, you have to maximize your strengths and minimize your weaknesses.

A good friend of mine tells a beautiful story of how he discovered his strengths and learned how to use them to his advantage. His name is Jim Kaat, and he's one of professional baseball's greatest left-handed pitchers. His tale takes place when he was pitching for the Minnesota Twins back in 1966.

The Twins had acquired a new pitching coach named Johnny Sain, who had been a great pitcher in his own right. Sain spent the first few days of spring training just watching his pitchers, taking notes, and not saying much. Finally, he called each of them in, one at a time, for a chat.

When his turn came to meet Johnny Sain, Jim Kaat figured he was ready. He'd been working like the devil on his full repertoire of pitches and was ready to learn from his new coach.

"Jim", said Sain, "of your four best pitches, which one is the best?"

Jim had been doing his homework. He'd been studying his pitches, and he could name the best one right off.

"My best pitch is my fastball. Then comes my curve. Next is my slider and finally, my change-up."

"What have you been working on this week?" asked Sain.

"My slider and change-up," said Jim. "If I can improve on those two pitches, I know I'll have a good season."

Sain looked at Jim for a minute and then shook his head.

"I don't see it that way, Jim. I'd like you to take a different approach. Your fastball is your best pitch. I want you to go out there in practice, warm-ups, and games and concentrate on your fastball. I want to see you throwing your fastball 80 to 90 percent of the time, all year, in every game. Do that, and you'll win a lot of ballgames."

Jim was stunned. It wasn't what he'd expected at all. He thought he'd get some technical advice about improving his curve or cleaning up his slider. But instead, Sain had simply told him to go out and do more of what he already did best.

Jim wasn't one to argue with his coach, especially one with a reputation like Johnny Sain's. As Jim tells it, "I saluted, clicked my heels, said 'Yes, Sir', and went out and pitched fastballs like you never saw. I threw so many fastballs I thought my arm was going to fall off."

But Jim's arm didn't fall off. And in that year, he went on to win 26 games and become pitcher of the year in the American League.

Now let me ask you the $64,000 question. Do *you* know what *your* fastball is? Do you even know what your best pitch is? If you do, have you been throwing it 80 to 90 percent of the time? Or are you spending your time in mediocrity by letting your God-given strengths and talents sit idle?

Thomas Edison was almost deaf. But he didn't waste valuable time trying to teach himself to hear. Instead, he concentrated on the things he did best: thinking, organizing, and creating. And he became great because of it.

Nobody has it all. Not you, not me, not Edison, Marconi, or Einstein. But people don't become successful because of what they don't have. They do it because they know what they have and they use it.

Every tennis star has a strength and an

exploitable weakness. John McEnroe, one of the world's best tennis players, has a slightly weak backhand. But you don't see him spending time doing backhand drills. On the contrary, you see him practicing that rocket serve of his over and over.

The same thing applies to business. Mary Kay Ash, founder of Mary Kay Cosmetics and one of the richest women in America, revealed in a recent television interview that she is perfectly helpless with numbers. Ask her something about her business that calls for an understanding of complex financial matters, and she generally says the same thing.

"Ask my son. He handles that department."

But ask Mary Kay Ash about making sales or recruiting new beauty consultants or about the things that motivate people and help them perform at the top of their game, and then stand back. Mary Kay Ash knows the secret to success. She leads with her strengths. She polishes her fastball, hones it, and uses it. And in doing so, she compensates for whatever weaknesses she has in other areas.

So how do you go about finding *your* fastball? The first thing you have to do is to get to know yourself.

Now that sounds pretty simple doesn't it? And if you were like me, your first response might be something like this.

"Hey, I know who I am. I'm Leo Hauser from Wayzata, Minnesota. I'm six feet two inches tall, have brown hair and brown eyes, and look pretty good if I say so myself. Yeah, that's me. Same guy who shaved himself this morning and the morning before that." No big surprises there.

But you also know that what we're really talking about is looking at your repertoire of pitches (your positive success attributes) the way Jim Kaat did, and finding your fastball.

I don't care if you're a banker, homemaker, student, or whatever. You're in business for yourself. Your success depends on your ability to satisfy your own needs as well as the needs of others. And to the extent that you give others what they want, will they in return give you the goods, services, emotional satisfaction, and positive results that you want and enjoy.

This is what's called the Universal Law of Reciprocity, and it goes like this. **The extent to which you give others what they want, will they give you what you want in return.**

"But wait," you say. "I should be getting more money from my employer and more love and affection from my family and friends."

It might be hard for you to believe, but what

you're getting today is exactly what you deserve. If your employer felt you were giving more of what he or she was looking for, you'd get more money and responsibility. And if you gave more love, respect, and attention to your family and friends, they'd be giving likewise back to you.

You might find this hard to believe, but it's true. And as soon as you accept it as being true, then you'll be able to start treating yourself as a business. And when you do that, you'll be on your way toward a successful future. You'll be able to look at yourself like any other business, whether it's a little corner grocery or the gigantic A & P grocery chain.

Ask yourself what it is that every business does at least once a year. The answer? They take inventory. They look to see what merchandise is selling and what's sitting on the shelf. They find out where they're getting a good return on their investment of time, effort, and shelf space, and where they're losing money.

Then they look at the merchandise that's not moving, the stuff that's just gathering dust and getting old. And they recognize that they're not getting a good return on their investment in those goods.

And what do they do when they discover

goods that aren't moving? Anyone who's been in business knows how selective they have to be about their inventory. If they have goods that aren't moving, they have an inventory clearance sale. They mark down the slow merchandise to whatever it will take to get it out of their store. That frees up time, capital, and shelf space. Then they take the money they get from their sale, and they invest it in more of the goods that are really moving. And that's what makes a business successful.

You have to do the same thing with your life. You have to take inventory of your strengths and weaknesses. And you have to build on areas where you're strong, and get rid of areas where you're weak. Like Jim Kaat, you have to find your best pitch and use it 80 to 90 percent of the time, in everything you do.

The first thing you have to do is to take a personal inventory of your assets and liabilities. You've got to take stock of what you have to work with in the "store" in order to figure out what's selling well and giving you a good return on your investment of time and effort.

TAKING INVENTORY

Honesty is what makes this exercise work. And sometimes, honesty is hard to come by.

None of us likes to look in the mirror and admit that the face looking back isn't that of Robert Redford or Jane Fonda. That's normal. But to make this first step work, you have to look critically at yourself and acknowledge your warts as well as your wonderfulness.

You're not going to write a piece of campaign propaganda or try to sell yourself to someone else. You're going to establish the foundation of your future success. As any good architect will tell you, you need a good foundation to build a towering skyscraper. The same applies to your own skyscraper of success that's got your name on it. It needs a firm foundation too. And you get that by taking a careful look at what you have to build your dreams on.

My approach to completing a personal strengths inventory isn't original with me. It was invented by B. Franklin, printer. That's right, Benjamin Franklin, creator of the lightning rod, the post office, and the lending library. He's the author of America's first inspirational self-help book, and he invented a surefire, stock-taking technique.

"There is no problem," said Franklin, "that cannot be solved with a pad of paper and a pen."

If Franklin had lived to see the automobile,

television, and stereo hi-fi, he might have added a third element; a quiet place to think. The Franklin/Hauser stock-taking system goes like this:

Concentration. Get away. Go someplace where you can be alone and can concentrate on your strengths and weaknesses. Get off by yourself. Go to a park, or get into a canoe and paddle out to the middle of a lake. But be sure to take along a pad of paper and a pen. And then resolve not to come back until you're finished.

Be Objective. Draw a line down the center of the first page. That's not too taxing so far, is it?

Terrific and Like. On one side of the page, write down all the things you like to do and are good at. Don't just limit yourself to those things you get paid for or that are hard to do. And don't put things down just because you think other people would want you to put them down. List things that are easy and fun, things that are hobbies, and things you never thought of as being work. If babysitting is a blast for you, write it down. If barbecuing is your thing and everyone raves about your Fourth of July special sauce, put it down. Just remember Colonel Sanders.

Lousy and Dislike. On the other side of the

page, list those things you're not very good at and don't like to do.

Don't be surprised if you find it easier to write a list of things you're not good at. Just remember that since kindergarten, when you were a little kid, you've been learning to criticize yourself and others. School and work? The same story, criticism. In fact, our whole culture is preoccupied with criticism. Turn on your television, and what do you see? Commercials telling you how bad you smell, look, taste, and feel.

Lots of people think of themselves as nothing but complete klutzes. So don't be surprised if after you've made your two lists you have five or six times as many bad traits as good ones.

Appraisal Time. Narrow down your list of attributes, talents, and skills to one or two things you are legitimately good at and like to do. Look for one or two items on your list that have earned you the applause of others in some way. Things you'd do whether you had to or not, even if nobody applauded. Those are the talents and skills that will make you the success you're destined to become. Hold on to them. Don't let them go. Together, they're your key, the ticket to your future. Whether you have one skill or several, when you put them together, they'll be your fastball.

DON'T PROCRASTINATE

Right now you're probably thinking that the Franklin/Hauser stock-taking system isn't so bad. You're probably saying to yourself, "It'll take some time, but I can do it ... as soon as I can get around to it."

You can come up with all kinds of excuses for not getting started right away. You might have used some of the same excuses for other things you've put off.

"I'll get started as soon as ... the vacation is over ... and the kids are back in school ... and that other project is done ... and I've finished Christmas shopping ... and the Superbowl is over ... and spring vacation has come and gone ... and we're through with little league ... and ... and ... and."

I'll level with you. I know that if you do this exercise you'll find your fastball. And you know you can do it. But honestly, I can't force you to do it. You're an adult, and you're going to have to decide what's best for you.

I can see the results of this little exercise in my checkbook and in the awards I have hanging on the walls of my office. I can prove to myself that these five steps to success work when I throw my arms around my marvelous wife Helen or our three wonderful kids, Polo, Libby, and Sara. That holds true for all five steps. You're just going to have to take my word for it and start doing them right now, not sometime in the future when you think it's convenient.

As they say in the appliance business, "If all else fails, follow the instructions."

Before you move on to step two in the FIVE STEPS TO SUCCESS, I want to give you something to gnaw on.

You've already come a long way, a lot further than most people. For one thing, you obviously care enough about yourself, your future, and your chances for success or you wouldn't have picked up this book. Just remember this. There are 250 million people in this country and your chances of success are just as good as everybody else's. Probably better, because you're unique. You're one of the few who care to, and dare to, succeed. Yet, you know it won't be easy.

IT'S NOT ALL CHIN INTO THE WIND

I won't kid you about it. Most of the successful people I have known, read about, and studied, have gone through a period of turmoil in which they questioned who and what they were. They never got around to working on

Step Number One until most of their options and alternatives for doing it the easy way had evaporated or proved fruitless.

Some of these people were financially broken. Some were alcoholics. Some had lost their families. Some were even in prison. Almost all of them were desperate. But regardless of how good or bad these people appeared to be, everyone of them clung to that final straw in life where the only thing left was prayer.

"Dear God," they pleaded, "isn't there one thing in me that matters? Isn't there one thing left in me that I can build on? I just want some dignity and productivity in my life. Isn't there one thing left that I can use?"

Then they went out and took their inventory. They found one or two true talents and they used them to put their lives back together, better than before.

And me? Yes, it happened to me as well. I wish I could tell you I missed my crisis in life, but I can't, because I didn't.

My moment of truth came on my thirtieth birthday. It was just a birthday, but it was one for which I had real big plans. You see, I dreamed, hoped, wished, and expected to be a millionaire by the time I was thirty. But not only was I not a millionaire, I owed $15,000 on my furniture, appliances and car.

Ever since I was young, when my dad told me to reach for the Great American Dream, I wanted to be successful. When I was old enough, I read every biography of every great industrialist I could find. I looked at those guys, I looked at myself, and I made a resolution.

"Hey, Leo," I said to myself, "you're every bit as clever as any of those guys. You're going to be a millionaire when you're 30 years old."

After having decided that, I went about my business. I got a job, got married, and started raising a family. We bought a house, two cars, and a color television. None of it was paid for, but I thought, "What the heck." My ship was due any day.

But when my thirtieth birthday arrived, my ship was nowhere to be seen. It wasn't even on the pond.

Was I surprised? You bet I was. After all, my father had convinced me that I could do it. I had studied all the winners and I knew their secrets. I was such a cocksure hot dog that I was even giving "get rich" advice to all my friends.

The realization that I was a damnsite short of any place I thought I'd be hit me in the stomach like a cannon ball. And it hurt. There

I was, sitting bolt upright in bed on my thirtieth birthday, whimpering like a kid with a hole in his pocket, watching the Good Humor truck fade into the sunset.

All this wailing and gnashing of teeth woke my wife. She rolled over on one elbow, cocked an eye, and gave me her most empathetic shot.

"What's going on?" she asked. "It's bad enough being married to an old man of thirty, but now I've got a crybaby to boot."

"No," I said, "you don't understand. I've never shared this with you, honey, because I know you'd think I was cuckoo. But here it is, my thirtieth birthday, and I'm supposed to be a millionaire. And instead, I'm making payments on my payments."

Mrs. Sympathy shifted into high gear.

"You're incredible," she said. "Do me a favor. Don't say anything about this to my folks. They think you're crazy enough as it is."

I tried to explain, but she cut me short.

"A millionaire," she said as she looked me in the eye. "Here you are, making ninety-five hundred at General Mills, not counting all the free samples you take home in your briefcase at night, and you're upset because you're not rich. I love you, tiger. But you're coming unraveled."

Well I moped around for a week, feeling sorry for myself and thinking I was a complete failure. Finally, I got mad, piled into my little Studebaker, and drove off to the park. I sat there with my pen and pad of paper in hand and started to take inventory.

About two hours later, I had two entries in the "plus" column. One was that I liked people and the other was that I was good at sales.

Now that may not seem like a lot to you, but after nearly thirty years of organized wishing and hoping, finding two positive attributes in two hours felt good to me.

It wasn't all fun and games, either. I'd been holding fast to a bucket of beliefs about myself that were just plain baloney. I had to step away from my own smoke and laser-light show, pull the plug on my electronic noisemakers, and do an honest search for my real tune.

We all have talent, something we do well and with ease. It's something we can hardly remember *not* being able to do pretty well. But many times we don't use the talent we have, and it must be used. The secret is to give it room, respect, and exercise.

Talents aren't necessarily big Edison-or Kissinger-sized things. An even temper, a skill at taking grief from other people, or just a sunny disposition are all talents. So are high energy, little need for sleep, and seeing work as fun. And there isn't a talent that you can't tune into or onto. It takes time, effort, peace and quiet, searching, modesty, and introspection. And you've got to realize that no matter how small, meager, or simple your talents may appear, they can work wonders for you if you want them to.

I'm happy I took inventory when I did. It wasn't a barrel of laughs, but it worked. It was a turning point in my life, and from the very start, it paid off. It allowed me to grab hold of my life, stop living in a dream world, and start living in a wonderful reality. It helped me come to grips with myself and see what needed to be done. And it made me persevere, to hold out for the real thing: Life with a capital L.

This is Step Number One of the FIVE STEPS TO SUCCESS. It's the foundation for whatever success you want in your personal or professional life. You have to get to know yourself.

So invest whatever time is required to take your own personal inventory on the next few pages. Give it the respect, time, and energy it truly deserves. Not for my sake, but for yours.

When you've completed your inventory and know what you're good at, then let's move on together to Step Number Two, PICKING THE RIGHT OPPORTUNITY.

RULES FOR EFFECTIVE PERSONAL INVENTORY TAKING

1. Make it a TOP priority - this is extremely important for you and your future.

2. Pick a date and vow nothing will interfere with it - just like meeting with your lawyer or minister on an important business or personal matter.

3. Plan on a minimum of 2 continuous hours.

4   Pick a quiet place away from people, telephones, TV or any possible interruptions or distractions.

5. Be rested and fresh - preferably, first thing in the morning, when your mind is clearest and has the least external pressures.

6. Have plenty of paper, pens and whatever else you may need to do the whole job in one sitting.

Congratulations & Good Luck!

STEP ONE — GET TO

MY "FASTBALLS"

STRENGTHS, TALENTS, ABILITIES, AND THINGS I LIKE TO DO

KNOW YOURSELF

MY "CHANGE-UPS"

WEAKNESSES, THINGS I'M NOT VERY GOOD AT AND I DON'T LIKE TO DO

ADDITIONAL THOUGHTS
AND INSIGHTS ON MY STRENGTHS
AND THINGS I LIKE TO DO.

STEP TWO
PICK THE RIGHT
OPPORTUNITY

Once you've found your fastball, you need a game to play in and chance to show your stuff. You need an opportunity to use the skills that are going to lead you to the success you're looking for. What you want, specifically, is a situation, job, activity, or way of life that allows you to feel good about what you're doing 80 to 90 percent of the time.

That simple idea of using your best pitch 80 to 90 percent of the time is my way of knowing that I've found the right opportunity for using my God-given talents. When I'm able to step back and see myself doing what I'm doing, right in the middle of doing it, and if I can honestly say I'm having a whale of a good time doing my thing, then I know I've successfully matched my talents with the right opportunity. It's the same criterion you should apply to your life to know when you're playing in the right game.

KNOWING ONE WHEN YOU SEE ONE

Most people can't tell an opportunity from an avocado. They're not trained to stand back and look objectively at the rich harvest of alternatives facing them. Instead, they've all been told "not to look a gift horse in the mouth", that "opportunity knocks but once", that they should "strike when the iron is hot", and that "he who hesitates is lost".

There's truth and wisdom in those sayings, but they're often used inappropriately to teach people to jump at every opportunity that comes up instead of objectively evaluating what's out there.

What do many people do when they leave school, get out of the service, lose a job, or for some reason or other find themselves with an indefinite future? They head for the nearest foxhole they can find and they hunker in for the rest of their lives, afraid to move.

Thoreau said, "The mass of people live out their lives in quiet desperation." And along those same lines, Mae West said, "Life is a banquet and most people are starving to death."

She was right, lots of people behave as if

they're about to starve to death. As if there's a shortage of success opportunities. They're so afraid of missing a car or house payment, so panicked at not having some place to go on Monday morning, so worried about not having playmates to bowl or fish or party with that they jump at the first likely paycheck. And the consequences of all that leaping without sufficient looking is tragic.

A Harvard professor by the name of Dr. Harry Levinson estimates that 80 percent of all working people are unsuited for the jobs they hold. Their talents are mismatched with their opportunities, which is the same as not having any opportunities at all. And the sharp edges of their ambitions are beaten needlessly into dull plowshares.

They might have been the right person for the job they now hold at the time they took it. But the job changed and they didn't. They refused to keep current with the new techniques of their industry, so they became virtually useless - like a fireman on a diesel locomotive.

On the other hand, they might have changed when the job didn't. Now the same old job routine is dull and boring. They've taken courses and read books that have ignited their ambition to do more creative things. They want a challenge, but they don't have the guts to quit their job and go with their fastball.

John Haney is a good friend of mine and an officer in a large bank. When he heard me talk about this problem, he quickly agreed. He went on to say that in his bank, they have two types of people who quit. There are those who quit and leave, and there are those who quit and stay. The ones who quit and stay are desperately unhappy with their job and its challenges.

Unfortunately, the latter group doesn't have the guts to leave. Instead, they just hunker in, refuse to grow, and complain about their lack of progress within the system. They completely refuse to recognize that it's their resistence to change that's at the root of their problems.

John went on to say that the people who quit and stay on are responsible for at least 80 percent of the bank's daily operating problems.

Is it any wonder that our society is ravaged by chemical dependency? That some people are preoccupied with tossing down and snorting up every variety of stimulant, depressant, or tranquilizer they can lay their hands on? Doing everything they can think of to anesthetize themselves to the fact that they're in the wrong place.

I have often wondered if the reason there are so many recreation vehicles is that people want to get as far away from their daily grind as possible. Out of sight, out of mind. But no matter how they choose to escape, many people want to spend as little time and effort (especially mental effort) on the job as they can. The job they were so eager to have has turned out to be a poor match for their talents, wants, and needs.

A group of industrial psychololgists asked several hundred people to make believe that they'd suddenly won a million dollars. The psychologists then asked the following question: "Would you continue to work?"

Over 75 percent said, "Heck, yes. Who wants to hang around all day doing nothing."

The researchers then asked those who said they would keep working if they would stay with the job they now had.

Ninety percent said, "Heck, no. I'd do something I could really get into, and I wouldn't worry about the money."

Then the researchers asked, "What would you rather be doing?"

Most of the people answered, "I don't know, but it would be something I could do well and feel good about doing."

In other words, these people would look for a job that would allow them to throw their fastballs

80 to 90 percent of the time.

Can you imagine all those people doing work they'd quit at the drop of a hat if they could only afford to? The bitter irony in this little story is that nobody is going to give those people the million dollars they need to make their dreams come true. And they're never going to earn that million. Not by working at a job that they don't enjoy doing. And certainly not by working at a job that is so disagreeable to them that they would rather be someplace — anyplace — else.

One of my favorite quotes is from John D. Rockefeller. "If your only goal is to become rich," he said, "you will never achieve it."

I agree. Your goal should be to match your talents to the right opportunity, whether it's a job, vocation, or mission in life. It should turn you on so much you can't wait to get at it. That's the way it should be, and that's the way it will be when you've mastered these FIVE STEPS TO SUCCESS.

So how do you find the right opportunity? One thing you shouldn't do is go around asking for advice. Relatives and well-meaning friends will love to give you advice about what you should be doing with your life. But they're usually just taking their own pulses. The advice you get from them is just a reflection of what *they* wish they would have done, could have done, or had the nerve to do with their own lives. Ask for advice and you'll hear something like this.

"You know, I often look back and wish I would have become a professional porcupine plucker when I was your age. That field is really blooming. Those porcupine pluckers are doing okay. Lots of room for growth in that porcupine-plucking business. They make a good penny, those pluckers. You know something? You could get into the plucking field. I can tell you'd be good at it."

It doesn't matter what particular field they're pushing, be it computer programming, frozen yogurt sales, or nude mud wrestling. It's got to be *your* field to be good, to be right for you. You can't wear the other person's boots, and they can't wear yours. You've got to be comfortable in your own.

In the last chapter you examined and evaluated your talents and skills and found the special few that will make you a success. Now comes the matching of those skills with opportunities.

ASSESSING YOUR HERE AND NOW

Before you march up to your boss and announce, "I wouldn't work for this chicken outfit another ten seconds if it was the last place on earth," you need to look around.

You have to be sure you aren't walking away from acres of diamonds because you're in a bad mood or are suffering from a temporary case of the blahs.

If you're in a job you've held for a year or eighteen months, you've been able to survive and learn the tricks of getting along. But to find out if the job is really right for you, do this simple little exercise.

Let's get started. Turn to and look at the headings of the next two work pages.

Good things. On the left-hand page, write down all the good things about your current situation. And remember, you're a proven pro. You know how to get a job, work at it, and hang on to it. Undoubtedly there are some good things about your job, some liveable spots you've built into your day-to-day routine. After all, you've survived by learning to understand and get along with a lot of different people. You know what to do when, and you know how to react to problems and get them solved. All of that counts for something.

So go ahead and write down all the good things you find in your current situation. Dig hard, be honest, and admit that there are some good things you're doing. If you're unemployed, you should realize you have free time on your side. That's not a joke, it's an important consideration. Some of today's most successful businesses were started during the depression of the 1930's by people who suddenly and unexpectedly had a lot of free time on their hands.

Bad things. On the right hand page, write down everything that bothers you about your job, all your grievances and complaints. If you wake up every morning with a knot in your stomach, if you get sick thinking about the day ahead, or if your mood gets darker as you near the front door of your shop, store, or office, write down why you feel that way.

STEP TWO — PICK

GOOD THINGS ABOUT
WHAT I'M DOING

THE RIGHT OPPORTUNITY

THINGS I HATE ABOUT
WHAT I'M DOING

Comparisons. Now look at your two pages. Do the bad things outweigh the good ones? Are you bored and just putting in time, or are you temporarily miffed at losing some little office skirmish? Are you mad because someone else got the promotion you wanted? Are you thinking of jumping ship just to "show them"? Are you willing to give up a lot of good things for a little spasm of bad temper? Are you walking away from "acres of diamonds" without ever bothering to bend over to see if they're there?

Think carefully about your answers to these questions. In politics, they say voters are sometimes inclined to keep devils they know rather than elect devils they don't. Sometimes that mentality carries over to job-hopping. The troubles you *have* with your job might be slight compared to the troubles you could *get* if you quit and looked for another.

If, however, you are 100 percent convinced that you're in a spot you've got to get out of in order to have a shot at success, then quit. But know for sure that the problem is *them* and not *you*.

How do you know if it's you or the situation that's making you hate every livelong working day? One way to make that decision is to simply be in touch with the way your stomach feels when your thoughts suddenly turn from play to work. Does your mood go from sunny to cloudy? Does the dark side of your personality come to the surface? Do your kids take two steps backwards, just in case? Can you feel your muscles tense and your brow furrow? If that's you when you're away from the job and you suddenly remember you have to go back again, then you've just cast one vote against stay and one in favor of go.

JOB ANNOYANCE RATING (JAR)

Here's another way to judge how your job situation affects you. Go back to your list of things you hate about your situation and read each item on the list. Then rate it according to the scale that's on the following page.

JOB ANNOYANCE RATING (JAR)

1	2	3	4	5
This annoys me some of the time.	Annoys me every time it happens.	This really irks me.	Makes me mad.	Makes me so mad I could burst.

Your list might look like this:

1. How my boss treats me 3
2. Big mouth Arthur 2
3. They never listen to me 3

When you've rated every item on your list, add the ratings for every item. Then divide the sum of the ratings by the number of complaints on your list.

$$\text{Number of complaints} \overline{\smash{\big)}\ \text{Sum of ratings}}^{\ \text{JAR}}$$

The number you end up with will be between 1 and 5. This is your Job Annoyance Rating (JAR). If your JAR is between 1 and 2, you're about average. Most situations are this irritating. If your JAR is between 4 and 5, you have an unusually irritating job. You might say your JAR is full. Strike two.

If your JAR is between 3 and 4, things aren't good. Don't jump ship yet, but don't dismiss the idea either. You still might have to later on.

Now for the crucial final test. Compare the list of good things about your situation with the list of your strengths and super strengths you made earlier, and answer the following questions:

1. Do my strengths (my fastball) match the good things about my situation? _____

2. Can I change or reshape my situation so I can use my strengths/fastballs? _____

3. Are the things I like about my present situation related more to the work than to the people I work with and the good times I've had? _____

If you answered "no" to two of the three questions, it's strike three against your current situation.

Once you've gone through this exercise and assessed your situation, you can decide either to (a) stay and work to improve your situation, or (b) go and look for something with more opportunity for success and more room for you to throw your fastball.

If you've decided to leave your current situation, skip the next section, MAKING THE MOST OF WHERE YOU ARE, and go on to the section called LOOKING FOR A

NEW LEASE ON LIFE. If you've decided to stay where you are, then read on.

MAKING THE MOST OF WHERE YOU ARE

Okay, let's start mining those rough diamonds and brightening your corner of the world. Here's where Ben Franklin's sage advice about pen and paper comes back into play a third time. The blueprint for your success consists of the two lists you made of your strengths and opportunities. I want you to make another list by following these steps.

What is Best? At the top of the next work page, write down the best thing about your present job.

Your Fastball. Right under that good thing, put down your fastball; your list of strengths.

Match 'Em Up. Now just let your mind go and scribble down everything you can think of in answer to this question: "How can I use my strengths to make this good thing about my present situation even better?"

Don't censor yourself. Write down every idea, no matter how silly or crazy it may seem right now. Go ahead, do it. Take about 10 minutes for each item on your list of strengths.

Next Best Pitch. Put down the next best thing about your present situation. Then go back to your list of strengths and write down how you could use each of them to make that good thing better.

Keep doing this for every good thing about your job that you can think of. Don't rush. Take whatever time you need. This is an investment.

MAKING GOOD EVEN BETTER

1. What I like best about my present job:

   My Fastball(s)/Strength(s)

   How this, together with my strength(s), can make my present job even better:

2 . Next best thing about my present job:

   How this, together with my strength(s), can make my present job even better:

Let's Evaluate. Now go back and edit your ideas. Think about each one. Underline the ideas you think you can actually accomplish. When you have a list of at least five good ideas for using your fastball, you're ready to make a plan for success. And that's the topic of the next chapter. But be sure to finish the rest of this chapter before you go on.

LOOKING FOR A NEW LEASE ON LIFE

This section is important only if you've decided that you've got to change your job situation to utilize your God-given talents.

Once you've decided to go, you have to decide where. To the next best foxhole like you did before? To a better, more carefully chosen job? On into business for yourself? The decision is yours to make, but here are some things to consider when trying to make that choice.

First of all, I want you to carefully think your way through your decision to look for another job or go into a business by yourself. Many people who go into business for themselves often do it for the wrong reasons. They say, "I'm tired of being bossed around. Now it's my turn." Or, "The owners have all the fun and money, so why not me?"

Can those attitudes have anything to do with the fact that 85 percent of all new businesses fail in two years or less? Many of the country's most successful businesses would never have gotten started if their founders had had the slightest idea of how much work it was going to be. Still, it's an attractive option. And it's one you have a perfect right to consider and accept or reject.

FUNDAMENTALS OF SUCCESS

Here are some things I know about starting and running a business. I learned them from my own experience and my observations of other successful people.

• Thomas Edison said that invention is one percent inspiration and 99 percent perspiration. That's true of success in any endeavor, especially in starting your own business. Success starts after 5:00 p.m. and on weekends. The difference between a job and a career is about 20 hours a week.

• Successful people invest in themselves. They go to seminars, read a lot, and consult with others. They are natural and eager learners. That doesn't necessarily mean they go back to school. They just believe that there's something to be learned from every encounter they have with other people and their ideas. And they make sure there are lots of those encounters.

• Successful people do not get involved with get-rich schemes. Whether it's a lottery ticket, a tip on a long shot, or a matchbook cover come-on, you can bet that really successful people will turn their backs on it. The reason is simple. Successful people believe they're in control of their lives and their fates. They know that effort means more than luck, that praying isn't a substitute for planning, and that pie in the sky is just dodo bird food. And you know what happened to the dodo bird.

Now don't misunderstand me. You'll frequently hear me say, "Let go and let God." I believe in that, because so many things have happened to me that I didn't - and couldn't— have planned for. I accept the fact that there is spontaneity in life; an element of the unknown and a power behind me. But I also know that no one ever succeeded by staying in bed all day waiting for their ship to come in.

A key point in one of my favorite inspirational books, Jonathan Livingston Seagull, is "He who flies highest, sees farthest." A surprising number of golden opportunities seem to open up for those people who work hardest at putting themselves on the success path.

Good luck is a loser's estimate of a winner's success.

• Successful people help others succeed. I've been—and am now—in business *for* myself. But I have never been in business *by* myself. I am only as successful as the people I help and who help me succeed. You can never do it alone.

The Bible says, "Cast thy bread upon the water." Now it doesn't say "Try it once, and if it works, good. If not, ..." No, it just says "cast". And like fly fishing, you have to cast and cast and cast to catch something worth keeping. The same goes for helping people. Successful people extend themselves to others, but not with the thought of immediate return. They know if they extend help to others, help will be given back to them sometime in the future.

• Successful people aren't jealous or resentful of other people's success. Successful people are *encouraged,* not *discouraged* by the good things that happen to people around them. To be angry over the accomplishments of others and resentful of their success is a waste of time that successful people can't afford, especially when they really believe in themselves.

My favorite religious hymn contains this theme, "Let there be peace, love, joy and

prosperity on earth, and let it begin with me."
And if I really feel that way, there just aren't
enough hours in my life to waste one split
second resenting another person's success.

• Successful people have supreme self-
confidence. They believe that their ideas are as
good as, if not better, than everyone else's.
They feel that if they're given an even break,
they'll win the medal, gain the gold, and over-
come every obstacle.

• Successful people believe the best investment they can make is an investment in themselves. After all, they're the best, brightest,
and hardest working people they know. If
they're going to gamble on an investment,
they're going to make sure it's an investment
in themselves.

That's how I feel about success in general
and what I know for sure about successful
people (entrepreneurs in particular) that I have
known.

LOOKING FOR OTHER OPPORTUNITIES

If the risk of starting your own business
seems too great, don't do it. But don't fall
into the trap of believing that working for
someone else makes you an automatic failure.
Not so.

You can be a success working for someone

else just as you can be a success working in your own business or being homemaker of the year. The key lies in applying the FIVE STEPS TO SUCCESS, not whether your name or someone else's name is on the door. Finding and using your best skills and using them in the best way possible is what really matters.

If you are a fabulous research scientist and are totally disinterested in sales or administration, you shouldn't go into business by yourself. However, if you decide you must and will, then get a partner who's good at everything you hate to do and whose talents compliment your own. Finding and using your best skills in the best way is what really matters.

Let's assume that you aren't going to start your own business but are going to be looking instead for a new job with a new and better set of opportunities. The critical thing is to use your list of strengths and weaknesses to assess the opportunities of the new job. Review the list of things that have made your current or last job unbearable. Use that list as a screen for danger signals in your new opportunities.

1. Don't quit your present job right away. Even though you hate what you're doing, you should have your new opportunities lined up and ready to go before you make your move.

You might find it hard to believe, but the best thing that can happen to a lot of people is to be fired. Really. Some people just won't let loose of a job they're poorly suited for until someone does them the favor of firing them. And I really believe that for some people, being fired could be the best thing to ever happen to them, something actually worth celebrating.

2. Your best move is to get your ducks lined up right now before you go ahead and fire yourself from an unsuitable job. Remember, the job placement experts tell us that the *best* time to look for a job is when you already have one.

3. Look at your hobbies. Is there a way to turn them into a moneymaking vocation instead of a satisfying avocation? Can you do it in the next 30, 60, or 90 days? In the next year?

4. Has anyone ever offered you a job? Can you go back to that person again and reopen negotiations? Might that person be a good source for leads to someone else?

5. Consider going to a career counselor. Fulltime professionals can give you guidance on new careers and tell you just how well you might fit into a different situation. But be careful. If you go this route, work with a young counselor. They are less cynical and

more inclined to give you credit for determination and desire.

SUCCESS IS AN INSIDE JOB

Regardless of whether you've decided to strike out on your own and form a company, change careers, or give the job you have another chance, success is never accomplished on automatic pilot. You're going to have to do things differently as well as doing some things you've probably never done before.

Success comes from using your talents in the best way you can. You have to stand alone on the pitcher's mound and throw the strikes. No one can do it for you. You do, however, need support. Every pitcher needs a catcher and a team to work with. And every team needs a coach. Your success will be supported, nurtured, and aided by many people to whom you must reach out and offer help, just as surely as they must reach out and help you.

In his inspiring book, Prescription for Tomorrow, Harold J. Cummings, chairman emeritus of Minnesota Mutual, the nation's fifteenth largest life insurance company, advises us that to live in peace within ourselves, we must give to others and go on giving as long as we live.

"You'll never give away more than you get

back," writes Cummings. "Please accept that as being infallibly true."

To Harold Cumming's words, I can only add a heartfelt "Amen."

But all that help and helping are more than mere generosity. The more you help others, the more willing they will be to help you find a place to stand and throw your fastball. It's the Universal Law of Reciprocity again. And it's the key to success in everything you do.

CAUTION

There's a 10 percent deposit to be made on your 90 percent opportunity. So I want to caution you not to expect a utopia, a place where you always get to do only what you want to do and are good at. You may be the world's greatest salesperson, and you might even be good enough to sell the tower back to Eiffel. But sooner or later you have to sit down and write up the order, negotiate the contract, and follow through on your promises.

You may be the brightest and most creative CPA in town, but you can't show off until you have someone to show off to. You can be better than H. and R. Block put together, but that won't do you or anyone else much good until you get out and drum up some business. People aren't going to come knocking on your front door Monday morning begging you to do your thing for them if they don't know who you are.

Whether you're in business for yourself or work for someone else, your standard of living, income, and satisfaction are all in direct proportion to the goods and services you provide others. That's the Universal Law of Reciprocity again, and it determines your take-home pay, your net worth, and the amount of success you enjoy. You are, in fact, your own business, whether you own a company, work for one, or don't work for pay at all. So accept the fact that 10 to 20 percent of what you have to do to be successful won't be things you like to do and are good at.

YOUR CHALLENGE

Your task is to find ways to get the 10 to 20 percent done efficiently and as quickly and easily as possible. Any time you spend over and above what is necessary to get those somewhat tedious or odious tasks done is time taken away from throwing your fastball. And that includes time spent lamenting, regretting, and stalling before doing the necessary nitty-gritty work you don't like to do. Do it and forget it. Then get on to more important things. That, by the way, may be the best piece of time-management advice you'll ever receive.

WHEN DO I START?

By now I assume you've found your fastball, a game to play in, and a team to play on. Your next question has to be, "When do I get started?"

You may be thinking that you should wait until all the lights are green or the economy is in full bloom. It's reasonable, but not right. You see, we can all find lots of excuses and get free advice from friends and loved ones as to why next year will be a better year for planning and working on success. Let's face it, if you haven't done this type of thing before, it can be darn scary. And that makes procrastinating very easy.

But if you've done Steps One and Two of the FIVE STEPS TO SUCCESS thoroughly and objectively, and if you really want to be successful, then you must decide to do your thing and do it now. Such a decision is never going to be any easier. There will be no right time. There will always be reasons for delay and keeping you dreams on "hold".

I'll never forget a piece of invaluable advice I got from Ronnie Brukenfeld, a friend and fellow member of the New York Stock

Exchange. I met Ronnie when I was a young lad just beginning to trade on the floor of the Exchange. He was many years my senior in age, experience, and wisdom. But he befriended me and became my mentor.

One day, I learned that he had established his firm in 1932, in the middle of the Great Depression. I was amazed and curious to know how in the world he could have decided to start trading stock at such a historically lousy time. From everything I'd read, life on Wall Street in 1932 was pretty grim. You had to keep looking up as you walked down the street to avoid being hit by a bankrupt broker who'd thrown himself out of a skyscraper window.

I'll never forget Ronnie's response to my question of how and when he got started. He stopped short, moved in real close, looked over his bifocals at me, and addressed me in a slow, deliberate voice.

"Leo," he said, "if you want to do something badly enough, it's always the right time."

For Ronnie, with his burning desire and deep commitment, 1932 was the right time to go into business. He went on to become enormously successful.

On this same point, a story even closer to home comes to mind. As I mentioned earlier, my father had always been of great help to me in my quest for success. But he ended up doing more for me than I could ever have imagined.

To help celebrate my thirty-fifth birthday, both he and my mother drove out from St. Paul to our home in Greenwich, Connecticut. It was a joyous period for all of us. They were pleased and proud of my progress, and I was delighted to share some of my successes first hand, such as our growing family, lovely home, and my Wall Street activities.

One evening, my dad and I were having a warm, relaxed chat in the library when he shared a dream he had with me. He proceeded to tell me that his secret goal for years had been to go into business for himself upon retirement. He went on to say that in just two short years he would have earned maximum retirement benefits from his job with the U.S. Government. Then he'd be free to start up his own full-time business making little wooden toys in his basement.

My dad had been making toys for years as a part-time hobby so he could make extra money to help put my brother and me through school. He bubbled with excitement as he described the way he would set up the shop and distribute the finished products.

I was delighted and pleased to see my dad,

who had worked 42 years for the same government agency and achieved his goals, now to be ready, willing, and able to become an entrepreneur and start his own business. It was quite an evening for both of us.

My mom and dad left a few days later and our lives returned to normal. But a few months after they got home, and before my dad could retire, my brother, Tom, called with the chilling and sad news that dad had died suddenly from a massive heart attack.

All during my trip back to St. Paul and through the funeral arrangements and burial service, that conversation in my library in Greenwich with Dad kept running through my head. He had taken the ball in his own end zone and by hard work, determination, and dedication, carried it all the way down the field to the five-yard line and was ready to score a touchdown. Ready to retire and launch a new career that had been his burning ambition for the last 20 years of his life. Ready to become an entrepreneur and be in business for himself. Making the most of his God-given talents and being deliriously happy doing it. But the game ended before he could make his dream come true.

I'm not in medical science, and I don't pretend to be clairvoyant, but I have a very strong feeling that if my dad had settled for early retirement and stopped going down to the post office on Kellogg Boulevard several years earlier to pursue his toy-making dreams, he would have added 20 years to his life. He also would have added loads of satisfaction to himself, my mother, our whole family, and certainly to his customers. He may have even become the Colonel Sanders of the toy industry.

As sad as that event was for me, Dad had once again given me a piece of invaluable advice. If you want to do something so badly that it becomes a persistent voice in your conscious and subconscious thoughts, then DO IT! Believe me, it will be so much better for you and everyone around you.

If you want to do something badly enough, take Ronnie Brukenfeld's advice and know that right now is indeed the right time to make your commitment and cast off from the dock. And once you've got that courageous act behind you, move on to Step Number Three, SETTING BIG GOALS FOR YOURSELF. It's where you're going to be able to build a target for your game plan, and it's the theme of our next chapter.

If You Want

To Do

Something

Badly Enough...

It's Always

The Right Time!

STEP THREE
SET BIG GOALS FOR YOURSELF

This chapter will help you decide where you want to go and what you want to accomplish with your life by helping you set goals for the future. The essence of goal setting is captured in this old German proverb.

"You have to take life as it happens, but you should try to make it happen the way you want to take it."

That's good advice, and a helpful thought to cling to as you chart your course toward success.

I'm fond of saying, "Let go and let God." It captures my belief that you can't plan for some of the best things that will happen to you in this life. But I believe just as emphatically in the words of Career Development Psychologist David P. Campbell.

"If you don't know where you're going," said

Campbell, "you'll probably end up some-where else."

You have to choose the direction you want your life to take. You have to set goals and be prepared to be surprised as well. Let me be very clear about the paradox involved in set-ting goals on the one hand and staying open to opportunity and surprise on the other.

I believe that life is a journey and not a destination, that joy is as much in the running as in the arriving. The key is to move in a positive fashion, in the direction of your hopes and dreams, through goals that are both prac-tical and powerful. So when I'm talking about setting goals, I'm talking about *great big* exciting goals.

How big should goals be? As big as the goal Michelangelo included in his prayers.

"Lord," he said, "grant that I may always desire more than I can accomplish."

Big, far-reaching goals have a way of pull-ing the best from us, of giving us the incentive to work harder, to focus on success and to maximize our efforts.

How big should your goals be? Let me answer that by telling you a story. This is a story about a woman with a humble origin who had great big dreams. A young Mexican girl got married at 16. Two years and two sons later, she was divorced and left to raise her family by herself. But she was determined to provide a life of dignity and pride for herself and her two sons.

After crossing the Rio Grande River with all her worldly possessions knotted in a simple shawl, she ended up in El Paso, Texas. She worked in a laundry for a dollar a day, but she never lost her commitment to build a respectable life in the shadow of poverty.

While she was working in Texas, she heard she could do better in California. So with seven dollars in her pocket, she and her two sons took a bus to Los Angeles.

She started out washing dishes and taking jobs wherever she could find them. And she saved as much money as she could. When she had four hundred dollars, she and her aunt bought a little tortilla shop that had one tortilla-making machine and a grinder.

She and her aunt were so successful at making tortillas, that they were able to open other shops. And when the aunt found the work to be too hard, this young woman bought her share of the business.

The years flew by, and before long, her little tortilla shops grew to become Romana's Mexican Food Products, the largest Mexican wholesale food concern in the nation, employing over 300 people.

Having achieved financial security for herself and her two sons, this brave young woman turned her energies to lifting the level of her fellow Mexican-Americans.

"We need our own bank," she thought. And before long, she and a handful of friends had founded the Pan-American National Bank in East Los Angeles. The bank was dedicated to serving the Mexican-American community. And today the bank's resources have grown to more than $22 million dollars with 86 percent of the depository of Latin-American ancestry. But this young woman's success didn't come easy.

The negative-thinking experts told her she couldn't do it.

"Mexican-Americans can't start their own bank," they said. "You're not qualified to start a bank. You'll never make it."

She quietly said, "I can and I will." And she did.

She and her partners opened their bank in a little trailer. But selling stock to the community posed another problem, because the people didn't have faith in themselves. And when she asked them to buy stock, they declined.

"What makes you think you can have a bank?" they asked. "We've tried for 10 or 15 years and always failed. Don't you see, Mexican people are not bankers.''

But she persevered, and today that bank is one of the great success stories of East Los Angeles.

Are you having trouble figuring out who our heroine is? You've seen her name many times even though you may not realize it. But don't feel bad, because there are a lot of other people who don't know about this success story.

After the Pan-American National Bank succeeded, our heroine, Ramana Banuelos, moved on to even higher achievements and became the thirty-fourth Treasurer of the United States of America. Her signature appears on millions of dollars of U.S. currency.

Can you imagine that? A little Mexican immigrant who had a great big dream and went on to become the treasurer of the largest financial entity in the world.

Today, Romana Banuelos, with all those fantastic credits to her name, is back in Southern California dreaming new dreams and setting new goals. And she's doing it with that special knowledge that *a goal is simply a dream with a deadline.*

We're talking here about the kind of goals that a school teacher in Milwaukee, Wisconsin had. Her dream was simply to be a part of establishing a country where her people could worship with freedom and dignity according to their conviction. She met her goal and then some.

Do you know who I'm talking about? Golda Meir. That's right. A school teacher from Milwaukee, Wisconsin who had a simple dream, a dream that she could be just a little part of something big. She went on to become Prime Minister of Israel and one of the great statespersons of her generation.

HOW BIG IS BIG?

How big is a big goal? It depends on where you are when you dream the dream and set the goal. For a millionaire, making another hundred thousand dollars is no big thing. It's not a big goal and not much of a dream. But for a little Chicano lady with a four-foot by four-foot taco stand, it's a whale of a wish.

I'll give you a simple test of your goals. If your best friends don't laugh at you when you tell them your goal, then it isn't big enough. That's true. And it's not just your friends.

I used to be part owner of a bank, and I always felt bankers were rewarded for being very cautious, if not down-right negative. So they also provide a good litmus for your goals and dreams. If you can explain your goal to your banker and he doesn't turn green (or worse yet, likes your idea and agrees with your goal), then you're not shooting high enough. It's a good indication that your goal is not imaginative enough or grand enough to keep you excited and motivated for very long.

If, on the other hand, your friends laugh nervously, slap you on the back, and shake their heads, or if your banker looks as though his backbone turned to wrought iron, or if your mother-in-law whispers to your spouse, "See, dear, I told you this would happen," then and only then is your goal big enough.

This country was founded on big dreams. Our founding fathers set big goals and dreamed of things that most people couldn't even imagine. I was reminded of that in a marvelous way during our bicentennial celebration.

I was walking through our family room one evening early in July. Our kids had the television on and were watching the *Tony Orlando and Dawn Show*. Tony was about to direct the audience in a happy birthday sing-along. The song he had chosen was called "High Hopes." He explained his unusual choice of a birthday salute this way.

"I believe this song is the real American

national anthem," he said. "We live in a country where we can become whatever we want to be. We can be as successful, happy, sad, mediocre, enslaved, or as free as we care to be as long as we work at it."

"Think of the words we're going to sing," he continued. "High hopes. High, apple-pie-in-the-sky hopes. That's the real American theme song. It tells us to get great big, impossible goals.

"Shoot for the moon," he said. "Go for it. Shoot for the moon, because even if you miss by a little bit, you'll still land up among the stars."

That's so important, I don't want you to ever forget it.

Shoot for the moon, because even if you miss by a little bit, you'll still land up among the stars.

As important as that is, the world tries to keep us from going for it. The six o'clock news tells us the Dow Jones is down 15 points, the price of gold has plummeted, and the only things on the rise are despair and unemployment. A couple of weeks of that, and is it any wonder that people fail to crank up their sights and shoot for the moon? Is it any wonder that they choose instead to shoot straight ahead, hoping to hit the barn door just so they can hold onto what they have? The problem is that if they aim at the barn door and miss, they don't end up among the stars. You know where they end up, and it's not nestled in star dust. Where I come from, it's called manure.

HOW REAL WINNERS SET GOALS

Real winners are people who set and meet big goals, dream big dreams, achieve, have high hopes, and shoot for the moon. They're people who acknowledge world problems but don't succumb to them in their own lives. Successful people not only set goals, but they commit them to writing. They go out alone in their little Studebakers, think deeply about what they want to accomplish, and then put pen to paper.

Successful people not only set big goals, they also set them in five-year increments. They pick five years because goals that fit a shorter time frame seem less exciting and challenging. On the other hand, ten years seems so far away. There's no urgency to get started right away. Five years seems to be best suited for significant personal goals.

Do you know where you want to be five years from now? If you do, write it down. Do you know what goals you want to be working on between then and now? If you do, write them down.

Decide what business you want to be in, what activities you want to be performing, and the amount of money you want flowing through the till. Decide what family, spiritual, physical and mental goals you want to achieve. Decide those things right now, and write them down. If you are ever to set and meet prideful, meaningful, and fun goals, the first step is to express them as clearly as you can and then WRITE THEM DOWN.

PROOF THAT IT WORKS

Just in case you think writing your goals down isn't all that important, I'm here to tell you you're wrong, and I can prove it.

A few years ago, a behavioral research team from the prestigious Harvard Business School took a random sample of 100 graduating seniors and asked each of them this question.

"Where would you like to be and what would you like to be doing ten years from now?"

Every one of those 100 graduating seniors told the researchers they wanted to be rich and famous. They wanted to be doing important things like running big companies or in some way affecting and controlling the world we all live in.

The researchers weren't surprised by the answers they got. Harvard teaches their students that they're exceptional and destined to lead. And they are, to some extent, for no other reason than the fact that they're at Harvard.

But even among those elite future leaders, something astonishing showed up. Out of the 100 students who were questioned, 10 of those young tigers not only wanted and expected to whip the world, but they had actually written clear goals describing what they wanted to accomplish and when. None of the other graduates had written down their goals.

Ten years later, the same researchers went back to those 100 graduates with an extensive survey. They found that the 10 students who originally had written down their goals and plans owned 96 percent of the total wealth of the entire 100-student sample. That means that those 10 graduates were virtually 10 times more successful than their classmates.

Wow! We might have expected 30 percent, which is three times better. Or maybe 50 percent, which is five times better. But 96 percent! That is truly amazing.

And, gentle readers, with that revelation and proof, I rest my case for the vital importance of writing down your goals.

BY THE YARD IT'S HARD,
BY THE INCH IT'S A CINCH

Once you've written down your five-year goals and are committed to them, the next steps you take are remarkably simple. But they're the key to successful application. "By the Yard It's Hard, By the Inch It's a Cinch," pretty much says it all.

The key to meeting success with your big, five-year goals is to simply cut them up into bite-sized, day-by-day "do-ables."

Here's how it works.

1. Divide your goals by five. When you divide five-year goals by five, you end up with what else? Five one-year goals. Now you know exactly what you must accomplish between now and this time next year.

2 . Divide your yearly goals by 12. Congratulations, you now have your month-by-month goals. You now know what you have to accomplish between now and this time next month if you're going to be on track with your five-year plan.

3 . Divide your monthly goals by four. Couldn't fool you, could I? You knew

this was coming. But all kidding aside, you now know what you have to get started on next Monday morning. And just so you have no doubt about what you're going to accomplish, go on to the next step.

4. Divide your weekly goals by 4, 5, 6, or 7. The number you pick as a divisor depends completely on the number of days a week you want to devote to attaining your goals. If you love seven-day weeks, divide by seven. If you believe five is fine, divide by five. The one you choose is up to you. But whichever you choose, the end product is the answer to that very tough question, "What do I need to do today to be successful?"

When you've followed this procedure through to the end, you'll be ready every morning to hit the deck running with your target firmly fixed. You'll be ready to follow your own yellow brick road of daily, weekly, and monthly goals to the emerald city of your fondest dreams.

Clearly stated daily, weekly, monthly, and yearly goals help you harness your personal power, focus your energy, and concentrate

your effort on the things you've decided will
lead to the personal success and happiness you
want for yourself. Developing small, manage-
able, day-to-day goals relieves you of the
anxiety that comes from continually question-
ing what you're doing.

If you constantly doubt what you're doing,
you'll always end up doing it poorly. But when
you know that what you're doing represents
the best use of your time, you do it faster, better, and with more enthusiasm.

Setting five-year goals and dividing those
goals into day-to-day do-ables can also surprise you. The process can help you determine
whether you're really shooting for the moon or
just aiming at the half moon carved on the
outhouse door.

Say, for example, that you're in sales and
you decide that you have to see 500 new people
a year to meet your dollar goals. Allowing for
weekends and holidays, there are approx-
imately 250 working days in a year. This means
that with just two calls each working day (one
in the morning and one in the afternoon) you
can reach your goal.

Two calls a day. That's all. All of a sudden
you can look those 500 sales calls a year in the
eye and say, "I can do better than that, a heck
of a lot better. Just watch me."

That's exactly what happened to me. I found that I could do my five-day weekly plan in three and a half days. So by the end of the third month, I was working on my fifth month. The act of setting my day-to-day, five-year goals took the mystery out of success and turned magic into movement.

Just remember the bottom line. By the Yard It's Hard, By the Inch It's a Cinch. And the key to success is for you to write down your goals and use them as guideposts and mileage markers for your journey to success.

KEEP IT VISIBLE

If you write down your goals and file them away, they aren't worth the paper they're written on. You have to keep your goals alive in your day-to-day life. In my case, after I had that catastrophe on my thirtieth birthday, I was determined to keep my eyes on my goals and to focus on taking the steps that would get me to my destination.

After a lot of soul searching and goal setting, I was still sure that I wanted to be a millionaire. But I was embarrassed by the big deal I made of being a shoo-in by age thirty and then missing it. So I cautiously wrote down thirty-nine as my new target for becoming a millionaire. And to help me remember what I was trying to accomplish, I did one more thing.

I took a 1922 silver dollar that I had been carrying around as a good luck piece and put my great big goal on it. That's right. I took it down to my basement workbench, put it in a vise, and used emery cloth to polish off the reverse side and prepare it for an inscription. Then I took it to a jeweler and had him engrave it with these words.

"I will be a millionaire when I am 39."

The jeweler must have believed me because I think he overcharged me for the job. But even if he had charged me a quarter of a million, it would have been a worthwhile investment because my profit margin would still have been over three quarters of a million.

I won't try to tell you that every morning, when I scooped my change and keys off the dresser, I looked at the silver dollar and gave myself a pep talk about getting out there and doing the day's duty. That would be a lie.

But I can tell you that there were many days when I was down and willing to take some time off and start over the next week. Times when I wanted to end the day with a lunch. But I didn't because of that silver dollar with a simple but awesome goal engraved on it.

I can vividly remember digging in my pocket

for telephone change or lunch money and coming up with that silver dollar. I didn't always stop and read it aloud, but consciously and subconsciously it always reminded me of the minimum progress I had to achieve each and every day.

I'm convinced that on more than one or two occasions that little reminder kept me doing what had to be done. With God as my witness, I am telling you that I never missed doing what I had to do each and every day, just the way I planned it.

I retired that 1922 silver dollar on my thirty-fifth birthday, four years ahead of schedule.

You know in your heart that goal setting works. The behavioral scientists know from their research that goal setting works. And I know goal setting works because it worked for me in my life when nothing else did. So don't procrastinate — DO IT! Not just because I suggested it, or because it has worked so well for others. Do it for yourself.

NOTES TO MYSELF
MY 5 YEAR GOALS

Personal:

Professional:

ON GOAL SETTING
5 YEARS FROM NOW - 19____

Mental:

Physical:

Spiritual:

84.

1 YEAR FROM NOW — ____/____/19____

(yearly goals)

Personal:

Professional:

Mental:

Physical:

Spiritual:

1 MONTH FROM NOW — ____/____/19____

(monthly goals)

Personal:

Professional:

Mental:

Physical:

Spiritual:

1 WEEK FROM NOW — ____/____/19____
(weekly goals)

Personal:

Professional:

Mental:

Physical:

Spiritual:

TOMORROW & EVERY DAY
FROM NOW ON
(daily goals)

Personal:

Professional:

Mental:

Physical:

Spiritual:

ADDITIONAL NOTES TO MYSELF
ON GOAL SETTING

STEP FOUR
WORK

If you'll take a moment and look back over the preceding four chapters, you'll notice I've made a lot of promises. I promised to share with you everything I've learned about success. I promised that if you'd take the time to find your fastball, you'd have a critical success weapon. I promised that if you'd pick your opportunities and set great big motivating goals, you'd be well ahead of the game.

But there's one thing I *didn't* promise you. I didn't promise that the road to success would be easy. Not on your life. Because intrinsic to every big accomplishment, implied in every success goal, is a very unpopular little four-lettered word. It's called work.

There's only one place where success comes before work, and that's in the dictionary.

You may be a certified genius with an IQ of

700. And you may be president of your local Mensa chapter. You may be as glib as Gielgud. But to be successful in meeting your goals, actualizing your plans, and fulfilling your dreams, you have to get out and boogie. You have to work.

Now I know this isn't a popular piece of advice. Not today in our era of expected entitlements. But the simple fact is that without the lubrication of elbow grease and a dose of the old-fashioned work ethic, the machinery of success is going to grind to a complete halt. It will affect not only our pocketbooks, but our whole way of life as well.

GOOFING OFF

For many people, "goofing off" has become a way of life. It's an entitlement many people have come to expect from their jobs. Robert Half, the employment specialist, said this in a 1982 essay about goofing off on the job.

"Goofing off," said Half, "is literally goofing up the American economy. Time thefts (goofing off) deal a severe blow to the nation's productivity. They also fuel inflation by raising the cost of goods and services."

Half came to this conclusion by asking executives of 312 firms to estimate the amount of time stolen by their employees every week.

Using their figures, he arrived at a weekly average of 4.3 hours per employee. He multiplied this by the hourly rate of $7.41 and came up with $31.86 per employee, per week, as the actual per person cost of goofing off.

Then Half multiplied the per-employee goof-off cost by the number of nonagricultural, private-sector employees in the United States. He came up with a whopping $120 *billion* as the total cost of goofing off. That's more than the total cost of all shoplifting, fraud, and criminal acts committed against private sector employers in 1981 alone.

Goofing off is a very insidious problem. It's found in taking a little longer lunch hour, leaving early and coming late, jawing with fellow employees for a minute or two, or taking a phony sick day. No big deal, you say? Wrong! Wrong! Wrong!

It's a $120 billion ripoff, and it can keep you from meeting your goals and dreams. To keep from goofing off, you have to go where your goals can be met and do what needs to be done so they can be met. That means hard work and lots of it.

PRESS ON

I'm fond of the old adage entitled "Press On." I've heard it attributed to everyone from

Abraham Lincoln to Herbert Hoover, so I'm not sure where credit really belongs. It's still a splendid summary of my feelings about success and effort. It goes like this.

"**Nothing in the world can take the place of persistence.**
Talent will not; nothing is more common than unsuccessful people with talent.
Genius will not; unrewarded genius is almost a proverb.
Education will not; the world is full of educated derelicts.
Persistence and determination alone are omnipotent."

I admit it's possible to have the good things in life without doing a lot of work. You might inherit a bundle of boodle. You could win the New York Million Dollar Lottery. You could hit on a big dollar slot machine. You could marry rich. You could simply luck-out. Some people do. But considering the odds, I wouldn't plan on it for the first thing Monday morning.

The fact is, I haven't found a way to make it sweat-free, and haven't heard of anyone else who has either. For me, and for everyone else I know who's made a success of their lives, hard work is what has done it for them.

Many Americans have this odd, unrealistic image of their rights and entitlements. Like a field of Aesop's fabled grasshoppers, they sing, "The world owes me a living, a living."

Perhaps the world has changed to where each of us is owed a minimum-effort, dry-underarm, five-day, or 35-hour week. And maybe we are all owed a comfortable income, a car, a house, 2.5 kids, and weekends free for softball, bowling, football, and picnics. But I seriously doubt it. And even if it's true and destined to be, that to me is not success.

Success to me is not an easy street to mediocrity. Success to me isn't nine-to-five for 35 years and then out to pasture. Success to me isn't a risk-free, worry-free, perspiration-free, minimum-effort way of life.

THE IMPORTANCE OF WORK

To me, work and achievement are irrevocably linked in a process that begins after five o'clock and on Saturdays. Not out of a misguided or quaint sense of the Puritan Ethic, but because I see it as a natural extension of the size and excitement of the goals I want to achieve.

Unfortunately, we've been so indoctrinated by the nine-to-five, or 35 hours a week doctrine that we don't even realize there are other options.

I recently came across a Twin Cities Magazine

article about George Tesar, a man who had become exceptionally successful in the retail jewelry business.

George immigrated to the United States from German-occupied Europe after World War II. He started from scratch and made extraordinary progress by any standards. This is what the article quotes him as saying.

"There is still gold in them thar hills (America)," said George. "Anything that someone wants to do can become a success story. There is big competition in America between nine and five. But before nine and after five there is no competition. People go home. If you work later, or give a little more than you expect to get back immediately, you can't help but win in America because so many people stand with their hands out saying, 'Gimmie, gimmie, gimmie.' They don't come and ask, 'what can I do for you, boss?' or 'What more can I do?'"

A great example of doing that just right is Curt Carlson.

This man has become a living legend in my home state of Minnesota. The son of a Swedish emigrant, he worked his way through school as a golf caddy, had three newspaper routes at the same time, drove a soda pop truck and sold college advertising to make it through the

University of Minnesota.

After graduation he went to work for Procter & Gamble as a soap salesman, where he became aware of the trading stamp concept. While still at P & G, he moonlighted, borrowed $50 and started up Gold Bond Stamp Co. This became the foundation from which the Carlson Companies have expanded world wide with annual revenues approaching $4 billion.

Today Curt Carlson is the sole owner of the 17th largest privately held corporation in America and personally ranks among the Forbes 400 wealthiest people in our wonderful country.

When it comes to work and success, I think he sums it up very accurately, when he refers back to his early days as a salesman for P & G and then Gold Bond: "*Every* day is a tough day to sell. If you work five days a week, all you do is stay even with the competition. The sixth day – that's the day you get ahead."

In my scheme of things, success and work are synonymous. Work isn't something to be avoided. It's something to identify with. I equate work with the nobility of achievement. Work is the process part of success. Success is both the journey and the destination, and work is the activity of succeeding.

Work is the critical difference between wishing and winning.

If the dreams you're dreaming, goals you're setting, and plans you're making aren't as exciting to think about as a weekend golf game or tennis match, or as lovely and warming to think of as your family and friends, then you may not have done as great a goal-setting job as you think you did. It's going to take concentration, time, and a lot of hard work to reach the success you set for yourself when you saw your mountain, set your goals, and wrote your objectives. So you'd better really love that dream of yours, because you're going to have to eat with it, sleep with it, and live with it twenty-four hours a day, every day of the week.

Harold Cummings, whom I referred to in Chapter 3, gives this advice on work. "If you want to leave your footprints in the sands of time, make sure you're wearing your workboots."

I hope you don't think I'm a killjoy, trying to convince you that success comes from slavish drudgery in service to neurotic-sized goals. What I am trying to do is dispel from your mind that unruffled, cool-countenance image of success that the underarm deodorant and hairspray commercials serve up.

I'm sure you've seen the television images of success. The heroes are usually seen lying in the sun, sipping something cool while making big deals from the Bahamas by phone. They're also seen swishing silently down Wall Street in chauffeured limousines, buying and selling companies and countries. These simple-minded scenarios make beautiful commercials, but they're as off base as they are glamourous.

The other day, an old friend from Greenwich, Connecticut, was in town and stopped by our home. We chatted for a while and caught up on what we'd been doing since we had last seen each other.

Then my friend got up, looked around at me and our home and with a great deal of enthusiasm said, "Hauser, you're the luckiest guy I've ever known. Everything always works out fabulously well for you."

After saying that, my friend walked over and gave me a warm pat on the back.

Well, I really appreciated the warmth, friendship, sincerity, and enthusiasm with which that compliment was paid me. I responded with a big "thanks" and a warm handshake.

I thought about those comments after we parted. Then I smiled to myself and thought how true the old saying is, "The harder I work, the luckier I get."

By many standards I'm very lucky. But by

many standards I'm also a darn hard worker. I internalize the FIVE STEPS TO SUCCESS and then go out and put them into action. I pour on whatever energy, work, perspiration, or combination thereof that it takes to make things turn out the way I want them to.

WORKAHOLICS

By the way, others have felt the same way you and I do about success. Thomas Edison, who was known for his ability to work hard for days on end, was neither dull nor poor. He said this about work and success.

"I never did anything worth doing by accident, nor did any of my inventions come by chance. They came by work."

In his lifetime, Edison was one of the most successful and fun loving people to be found. But he was also one of the hardest workers.

Benjamin Franklin, America's first certified genius, was well-known for hard work, hard play, and a goodly measure of success. He also had a way with words. His alter-ego, Poor Richard, had this to say about success.

"In order to succeed, you have to handle your tools without mittens."

The man who discovered electricity in lightning; invented the potbelly stove, the bifocal, the post office, the lending library, and life insurance; and wrote Poor Richard's Almanac (the world's first self-help success book), clearly believed in work and fun.

Today, people who are eager to strive and succeed like you, me, Franklin, and Edison are called *workaholics*. The term surfaced in the indulgent sixties to give comfort to those who felt the world owed them the lifelong option of sniffing the daisies, chasing butterflies, and baying at the moon.

You remember the period. The Zonker Harrises of our society said it was beneath human dignity to dedicate themselves to a cause as mundane and potentially insensitive as working for some profit-making organization. They felt it was okay to go to school forever, to always be involved in the closest social cause, or to suffer some existential anxiety known as "trying to get one's head together." They also felt it was okay to simply do nothing. What was not socially acceptable was to enthusiastically spend one's time and energy in a commercial effort. Those who did were branded workaholics. They were considered lowbrows, and they were looked upon as being neurotic, if not actually psychotic.

A few years ago, Dr. Marilyn Machlowitz wrote a book called WORKAHOLICS. It was based on her Ph.D. dissertation and a series of articles she'd done for the *New York Times*. Her subjects were people who were considered workaholics.

Her findings surprised a lot of people. She found that workaholics are people who work a lot, like what they're doing, and enjoy the heck out of using the tools of their trade. She found no evidence to indicate that hard working people are psychological deviates who are automatically prone to "Type A" behavior, stress-related illnesses, or heart disease.

Eugene Jennings, a management professor at Michigan State University did a similar study of highly successful executives. He asked each of them if they were happy. Those who answered "yes" were those who generally worked 60 hours a week or more. But not only were these executives happy, they were also free of alcholism and did not have an unusually high divorce rate.

I don't think the problem lies with the so-called workaholic; the person for whom an hour of work seems like fifteen minutes, who honestly enjoys what he or she is doing, or who feels the way Betty Rollin did when she wrote her book, Am I Really Getting Paid For This?

To me, the problem lies with people who call the eager beavers "kooks" and who rationalize their own discomfort, boredom, and lack of accomplishment by calling the hard worker a neurotic or a workaholic.

So the next time you hear yourself being called a workaholic, consider it a compliment. And remember, the workaholic is both a rare and lucky individual. Because only the fortunate few have a vocation that is as much fun as a vacation.

SELF-MOTIVATION

I know there are bad bosses and companies that regularly stick it to their employees. So I won't try to tell you that all the discrimination suits, grievances, and unfair labor practices charged against American companies are just a tissue of lies or the result of poor public relations. That would be a disservice to the great social reformers of this country. But I still honestly believe that hard work fosters the process of psychological reciprocity.

The Universal Law of Reciprocity that we talked about earlier states that to the extent we give others what they're looking for, will they in turn give us what we're looking for. Its application in employee motivation is well known, especially by psychologists like David Berlow. Dr. Berlow likes to give short speeches to managers.

"I only know three things about motivation," says Dr. Berlow. "Find out what the employee wants, figure out how to get what you want through his getting what he wants, and then work like hell to see that he gets what he wants."

The formula works both ways. To get what you want from your boss, client, or someone close to you, apply the Law of Reciprocity the other way. Figure out what the other person wants, decide how you can get what you want from their getting what they want, and then work like hell to see that they get what they want.

Remember the law, because it's important. To the extent that you give others what they want, will they in return give you what you want. And to get the best results, you have to work hard at giving others what they want, and you have to give them what they want right away.

A FINAL WORD ABOUT WORK

Work is a direct investment. When you stop working, the return on your investment dries up. And that's easily forgotten once you start experiencing success. The early victories, the first breath of success, and the pats on the back from family and friends can all be seductive. Those good feelings can cause you to lay back and start living it up. And then you get into trouble. One way to get into trouble is to believe you don't have to keep pumping the handle to keep the successes coming. People will ask you to give a free talk or contribute your wisdom for the benefit of others. That's seductive, especially if the cause is appealing. But you can't do too much of it or the amount of time you spend on your goals will diminish. So you have to keep pumping if the trickle of success is to ever become a stream.

Another seduction is the lure of the fast buck. When you start to get successful, people will come to you with all kinds of hot tips and inside information. And every one of these favors and tips will end with an appeal for cash. You'll be tempted by the illusion that the "big guys" do it with mirrors and magic and not with hard work.

"I like your style," say the leaches. "And I'm going to help you make it really big. We'll put your money in fandangos, pal, and then we'll really go places together."

Just remember, when you start experiencing success, that's the time to double your effort and put the pedal to the metal. It's not the time to take your foot off the gas and start reading the Burma Shave signs.

Remember Andrew Carnegie's favorite piece of advice.

"Put all your eggs in one basket — and watch that basket."

A very good friend of mine, Bob Conklin, very successful businessman and author of many well known self improvement programs and books, is fond of an axiom that is so very appropriate in this area. It goes like this.

Very often, when people become successful, they stop doing the very things that made them successful in the first place. Don't fall into the same trap.

Work is the Fourth Step in the FIVE STEPS TO SUCCESS. Plan on it, respect it, and never be seduced into believing that it was your genius, talent, or good looks that got you where you are. It was the hard work and muscle you put behind your fastball. The people who tell you that you deserve to goof off and take it easy don't understand the difference between working to live and living to work.

Have you ever noticed how the unsuccessful people say, "Thank God it's Friday," while the successful people say "Oh God, it can't be Friday already." The two of them obviously have different dreams and goals and march to the sound of a different drummer.

Every day brings a new challenge and a new

chapter in your success saga. Renew your zeal for your goals, gather your faith, and build your strength every time you go to pitch your fastball. Don't apologize or feel sheepish about a little perspiration. It's the daily testament, hourly medal, and vivid proof that every day, in every way, you're doing a little bit better.

That's the end of my sermonette on work, the cleanest four-letter word in the English language. The rest is up to you. You've got to decide to run, throw, or punt. To take up the challenge or look for an easier way. And if you believe as I do, that the only place where success comes before work is in the dictionary, I'll make you this ironclad promise.

Work hard, and you'll never have to apologize to anyone (especially the person you see in the bathroom mirror) for anything you get, any goals you reach, or success you earn. Get out there and boogie and you'll own the most important thing in life: the self-respect and dignity that comes from hard work. You'll also enjoy the inner peace that only comes from knowing you did it the best way possible: your way.

NOTES TO MYSELF ON WORK

CURRENT WORK HABITS AND TECHNIQUES I WILL CONTINUE TO USE:

NEW WORK HABITS I WILL DEVELOP TO REACH MY GOALS:

STEP FIVE
HAVE FUN

"Wait a minute," you're probably thinking, "a chapter called 'Have Fun'? After that stirring sermon on the virtues of hard work? Leo Hauser has to be the last guy in the world who appreciates a good time."

I'll bet you think I must be some sort of a pain fan. If it hurts it must be good for you. No gain without pain. All that hurt-o-mania sort of thing.

Well, my friend, nothing could be further from the truth. I see no contradiction between the way I feel about work and having fun. In fact, I think the two are logically connected.

One of the biggest kicks I get is to sit back, look at my progress, and delight in my accomplishments. I'm having the time of my life, and I'm completely in charge of my fate. At least as much in charge as any human being can be.

I'm like a kid in a candy store or a dog in a butcher shop whenever I see things falling in place for me. I'm having a ball and I love it. You can feel that way too.

Once upon a time, I really did think success had to hurt and be grim to be right. But I eventually found out that while I had to think a little deeper, plan more carefully, and work a little harder to succeed, the pay-off was just fantastic.

The same thing will happen to you. You'll find your life will never be the same once things start working out for you. You'll go bananas when your Walter Mitty world becomes a reality. It's like being an astronaut on a trip to the moon. It's exhilarating. It's finding out that you're finally doing what you've wanted to do your whole life. My friend, nothing is more fun than that. I promise.

THE FUN OF SUCCESS

There's an extra benefit in being a success. Successful people live longer than other people. That's what the medical scientists tell us. And there are several reasons for it.

Successful people don't suffer from anxiety and depression day in and day out. They don't sit around anesthetizing themselves with booze and pills to hide from the jobs they don't like. They don't burn themselves out by living a life full of anxiety and fear.

Henry Ford lived into his nineties. Grandma Moses was still painting at 100. Albert Schweitzer was still operating a hospital in Africa at 89. George Burns won his first Oscar when he was 80. And when John D. Rockefeller died at 93, he was making a million dollars a week. And that was when a dollar was a dollar.

Rockefeller was so active that I bet they probably had to nail his coffin shut. But then I wouldn't want to go either. Not if I was making that kind of money. Would you?

Marc Chagall, a famous contemporary painter, celebrated his 95th birthday on July 7, 1982. When asked his personal motto for happiness and long life, he said, "Work, work, and more work." According to his wife, Valentina, Chagall still spends most of his time in his studio, working on his paintings, which is what he likes to do best.

Successful people are exhilarated by the quest for success. They get so enthusiastic and excited that their whole metabolism changes. New plans and ideas simply pour out. As they move into a higher state of excitement, they develop a closer harmony between their work and their goals. They operate at a totally different level of energy and existence than the "nine-to-five", "thank-God-it's-Friday" crowd. Successful people have found that doing something, and doing it well, provides its own rewards.

You'll discover the same things as your successes grow. You'll discover the continuing sense of fun and excitement that's spawned by your enthusiasm for what you're doing. It'll come from knowing that what you're doing is what you really want to do and are good at. With doubt and uncertainty behind you, and with clear and meaningful goals in front of you, your talent and innate genius will be free to soar. And before you know it, you'll be as highly involved with what you're doing as any star athlete, great scientist, famous artist, financial wizard, religious leader or successful land baron that ever lived.

At this point, you must be thinking, "That's a long road to success. I want to have some fun while I make my million."

Good! That's another characteristic of highly successful people. They're able to reward themselves for progress, no matter how slight. They recognize that every step forward is a step toward greater satisfaction. And they reward themselves all along their journey.

Dr. Frances Stern, a psychologist who works with burned-out salespeople who are suffering stress, emphasizes that we need to get high on ourselves. She feels that good, hard, honest work must be rewarded if it's going to be repeated. And if you keep doing what you do best, you're bound to be successful.

Work becomes play when you enjoy it so much you'd do it even if you weren't getting paid for it. That's one of the keys to the FIVE STEPS TO SUCCESS. Enjoy your work and have fun. But don't forget to take the time to be good to yourself. For example, after you set a daily or weekly goal and make it, you should feel good. You should allow yourself to have a good time. You've done something to be proud of, so you should pat yourself on the back. Buy yourself a present or take yourself to the movies.

Let others make you feel good too. Nothing is as demeaning as false modesty. When you do something good, other people will want to tell you that you're great. Let them. Don't be like the people who reject compliments and ignore kind words. If you do that long enough, you'll stop believing that you really have done something good. Then you'll stop trying and that certainly would be a grave mistake.

When other people tell you that you've done a good job, say, "Thank you. I really appreciate what you're saying." You deserve their compliments. And they deserve the opportunity to give them to you.

There will be times when you'll do something fantastic and there won't be anyone around to see you do it. That's too bad, but what the heck. Reward yourself anyway. Pat yourself on the back, buy yourself an ice-cream cone, and tell yourself how great it is to be you and how wonderful it is to have and achieve significant goals. No one can be better at giving praise or deserve it more than you.

Sometimes you're going to have to walk away from your work no matter how much fun you're having. That'll happen whether you think you need to or not. There are three reasons for giving yourself some quality time away from your work. They are your health, mental freshness, and the happiness of your loved ones. These, by the way, are some of the factors Dr. Machlowitz found to be associated with the happy people she called "workaholics."

To stay healthy, to keep your creative juices flowing, and to ensure the continued support and love of your family, you've got to know when to stop and smell the flowers, just as you need to know when to dive in and make things happen again.

TAKE CARE OF YOUR HEALTH

It's a known fact that successful people are healthy people. They feel good about themselves psychologically. And they don't suffer from anxiety and stress when they do the things they want to do and are good at. That's because successful people have a great sense of self-esteem, and they believe in the things they're doing. They also take care of their bodies. They eat right to keep trim, exercise to keep fit, and work to stay in good health.

Look around you at the successful people in your life. They know that to get the most out of life they have to be at their mental best. They enjoy their leisure and they go all out at having fun. But they also know that to enjoy their leisure and still meet their goals and dreams, they have to be physically and mentally fit, and you should do the same.

You should take the time to preserve the machine that holds and nourishes your spirit and fuels your fun. When it works well, you'll work well.

LIVE LONGER

A sound mind and body are an advantage for everyone. But you need something else. This was pointed out to me by my daughter, Libby, who's aspiring to be a doctor. She found an article in the *Boston Globe* in which a psychologist named Peter L. Brill emphasized the importance of being in the right job. Dr. Brill stated that the key to personal self-esteem and well-being was a sense of competency.

He concluded that working at the right job was more conducive to longevity than diet, exercise, or heredity. So if you're working at the right job, living by the FIVE STEPS TO SUCCESS, and taking care of yourself, you should outlive Methuselah.

STAY MENTALLY FRESH

No matter how well you're doing what you want to do, you can do it better by exposing yourself to interests and ideas outside your immediate, day-to-day activities. It works like this. The ideas, problems, and solutions you encounter will spark your imagination and give you ideas you can use in your own work. This phenomenon is called "problem solving by analogy" by those who study problem solving and decision making.

The first hot-air balloon was designed by the LaGoffiere brothers after they saw bits of charred paper floating up their chimney.

Leonardo da Vinci and the Wright brothers got their ideas about airplanes after watching birds in flight. Newton supposedly developed the laws of gravity after he saw an apple fall.

The key to problem solving by analogy lies in seeing something work in an environment that is foreign to the one you're working in, and then asking "what if" questions.

Many of the things medical scientists know about the human body were learned by asking "what if" questions. "What if blood flows through the body like water in the aqueducts of Rome?" asked Marcello Malpighi, the Italian physician who eventually discovered the vessels and arteries of the circulation system. "What if the nervous system acts like a telephone switchboard?" asked someone else. "And what if the brain works like a computer?" wondered another.

Each of the "what if" questions led to a new discovery. And each question was raised when the problem solver was exposed to something that was unfamiliar, a part of another world.

Have you ever noticed the way your mind works? It's a wonderful problem solver, but you'll find it sometimes quits working on tough problems and goes and does something else. You start thinking about something totally different, and this gives your mind a chance to work on the unsolved problem without interference from the things that are really bothering you.

I have never failed to get at least one (and sometimes several) super, creative, and wonderful money-making ideas when I'm on vacation. It usually takes me several days to unwind and stop thinking of the memos I should've written and the calls I should've made before I left. But once that's behind me, I'm into deep, rich, creative pay dirt.

The time you take to explore with your mind is not time spent goofing off. It's productive time. You expose yourself to quality diversions that refresh and enrich your thoughts. You should pursue these thoughts every day. You should broaden your view of the world and extend your areas of interest beyond your work.

Get your head out of the sand and think about, read about, and concentrate on something other than your work, regardless of how much pleasure your work is giving you. You can be more creative, productive, and efficient by expanding your horizons. Do it, and you'll find that variety is the spice of success and the key to enjoyment in every aspect of your life.

SPEND TIME WITH YOUR FAMILY

Time with your family tends to keep your whole life in proper perspective. It renews and maintains the most critical element life can give; loving and being loved. As important as your work is and as much fun as it must be for you, it's only a tiny, insignificant twitch in the universe we live in.

Your work might be fantastic. It might even turn out to be the kind of work that will have a tremendous impact on humanity. Henry Ford, Thomas Edison, Albert Einstein, and Madame Curie all led lives that changed mankind in great big ways. But the majority of us will never scale such heights, nor would we all care to.

So, no matter how good you want to become or how much you want to achieve, it'll be a hollow victory without the good will and love of those who are close to you. You might win the battle, but it will be at the cost of everything worth striving for. Success cannot come at the expense of the people you love.

As joyful as your work is, and as important as your achievements may be, they'll never be enough on their own to completely sustain you. Your loved ones might not be interested in your work, or they might not understand what it is that you do. But that shouldn't keep you from making a special space for them in your life.

You only go around once in life, so you want all the gusto you can get. Just be sure to take your loved ones along. Because without them, it's not a trip, it's a stumble.

WRITE IT DOWN

This is the end of Step Number Five. The chapter has been short and sweet, and I've tried to make it very logical, just as it should be. When you've done the first four steps with all your ability and enthusiasm, you deserve something that's simple and direct.

Please don't make the mistake of skipping over this chapter too quickly or without the same concentration you invested in the previous steps. Rewards and positive reinforcement are very necessary ingredients in any forward progress toward success.

Spend some quality time concentrating on the fun you'll enjoy in each of the major areas of your life. Then write them down on the next two work pages and refer to them just as religiously as you do with the previous exercises. It will put fuel in your tank.

If I've Done

The First Four

Steps Correctly,

I Deserve To

Have FUN...

And I Will!

NOTES TO MYSELF

AND WHAT I

Personal:

Professional:

ON HAVING FUN

ANTICIPATE ENJOYING

Mental:

Physical:

Spiritual:

Additional Notes To Myself

SHOOT FOR THE MOON

Well, friend, you now know the FIVE STEPS TO SUCCESS. I call you friend because we've traveled through each page and exercise in this book together. That in itself means you are indeed a friend and a person who, like myself, is dedicated to maximizing your God-given talents and abilities.

We've separated ourselves from the window-shoppers and tire-kickers, who are forever looking and talking, but don't have the guts or commitment to do the necessary things we've discussed in this book.

By reading this far and doing the suggested exercises you are now in a realistic position to SHOOT FOR THE MOON.

WHAT YOU SEE IS WHAT YOU GET

As you crank up your sights and prepare to shoot for the moon, please keep this in mind.

What you see is what you get.

If you see success, mediocrity, or failure in your life, that's what you'll get. In order to be successful, you first have to see yourself as successful. You have to cleanse your mind and expectations of any past disappointments, failures, or low self-esteem you might have been carrying around with you.

If you've taken the contents and suggestions of this book seriously and completed the exercises, then you're on your way to a happy future. You know what your fastball is, and you're looking forward to the successful results these five steps will deliver. You're consciously and subconsciously expecting success.

Each and every one of us has in our minds a giant television screen that operates twenty-four hours a day in the midst of activity, in quiet times, and while we are asleep. A soap opera plays on that screen, and we're the star. How we picture ourselves on that screen is exactly how we're going to end up our lives. No richer, no poorer, no happier, no sadder. What you see is what you get.

To make the play you star in and the real life you lead everything they can possibly be, write your goals and dreams and wishes down. Turn those big plans into day-to-day steps. Then see yourself accomplishing the personal, career, financial, mental, physical, and spiritual goals that give your life continued meaning. Throw yourself into it, and you'll have more fun than you've ever had before.

Remember, a mind once expanded by thought can never shrink back to its original size. My fondest wish is that the thoughts and ideas we've shared in this book will expand your hopes and desires and make your life just a little bit better. I hope that the FIVE STEPS TO SUCCESS will help you achieve the success you've planned for and deserve. I hope too that these five steps will help you live the life of satisfaction, contentment, and joy you truly want.

When asked what he wanted to be when he grew up, Charlie Brown of Peanuts fame said, **"I want to be incredibly happy."**

Using these FIVE STEPS TO SUCCESS, you, like myself and the many people before us, will indeed be *incredibly happy*.

So have a great life; you deserve it. SHOOT FOR THE MOON, you've earned it. And at the very least, I'll see you up among the stars!

INDEX

INDEX (con't)

INDEX (con't)